EXAMS

D0031951

F IN

EXAMS

The Very Best Totally
Wrong Test Answers

Richard Benson

CHRONICLE BOOKS
SAN FRANCISCO

Contents

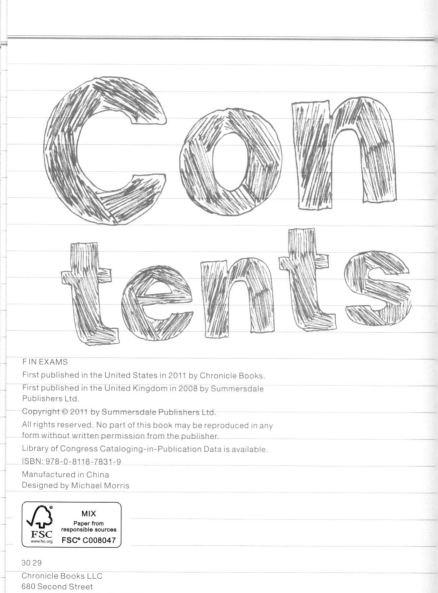

F IN EXAMS

First published in the United States in 2011 by Chronicle Books.

First published in the United Kingdom in 2008 by Summersdale
Publishers Ltd.

Copyright © 2011 by Summersdale Publishers Ltd.

Library of Congress Cataloging-in-Publication Data is available.

ISBN: 978-0-8118-7831-9

Manufactured in China
Designed by Michael Morris

MIX
Paper from
responsible sources
FSC
www.fsc.org   FSC® C008047

30 29

Chronicle Books LLC
680 Second Street
San Francisco, California 94107
www.chroniclebooks.com

Introduction

Pop quizzes, midterms, final exams—whatever the test, every student has experienced that terrible moment: You're sitting at your desk, classmates all around you, test paper in hand, staring at the next question and drawing a total blank.

Maybe you are a student now, putting off studying for the big test tomorrow by reading this book. If so, you won't find any useful answers. What you will find are hilarious, real responses from students who realized that they had no hope of answering a question correctly, and decided to have a little fun instead.

Whether you're still in school or you've come out safely on the other side, we can all agree that while the spectacle of failure can be highly entertaining, it's even better to see a FAIL turn into a WIN.

Subject: **Chemistry**

What is a nitrate?

It is much cheaper than a day rate.

Give a brief explanation of the meaning of the term "hard water."

Ice

What is a vacuum?

Something my Mom says I
should use more often.

What is the process for separating a mixture of
chalk and sand?

It is a process called flirtation

What is the process in which steam turns into water?

Convesation

What is methane?

Methane is a smelly greenhouse gas that is produced when trees and/or cows are burned.

What is the meaning of the term "activation energy"?

It's what is needed to get up in the morning.

In a blast furnace it is impossible for aluminum to be extracted from its ores. Why?

Because it is frickin' hot!

What type of attractive force or bond holds the sodium ions and chloride ions together in a crystal of sodium chloride?

James Bond

Over the last 50 years there has been a significant change in the concentration of carbon dioxide. Give a reason for this.

It's easily distracted.

What are the characteristics of crude oil?

Coarse and rude

Describe the chemical differences between H_2O and CO_2.

H_2O is hot water,
CO_2 is cold water

What is a vibration?

There are good vibrations and bad vibrations. Good Vibrations were discovered in the 1960s

What is the difference between a hydrocarbon (such as ethane) and an alcohol (such as ethanol)?

Hydrocarbon doesn't cause car crashes.

The burning of fossil fuels that contain carbon produces a gas called carbon dioxide. Draw a "dot-and-cross" diagram to represent carbon dioxide.

lemonade! ———>

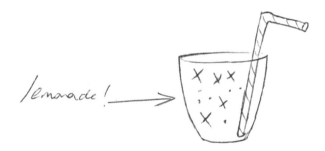

Subject: **Biology** ....

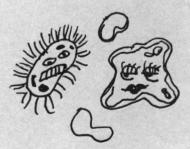

What is the lowest-frequency noise that a human can register?

A mouse

What is the highest-frequency noise that a human can register?

Mariah Carey.

Adam cuts his arm. Blood gushes out and is red in color. What does this show?

He is not a robot, he's a real boy!

What is a fibula?

A little lie

What is the meaning of the word "varicose"?

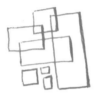

What does "terminal illness" mean?

when you become ill at the airport.

Define enzyme.

SUPERHERO OF THE CELL.

Define coenzyme.

ENZYMES' sidekick.

What happens during puberty to a boy?

He says goodbye to his childhood and enters adultery.

Give an example of a smoking-related disease.

Early death

What are the three different types of blood vessels?

Vanes, anchovies and caterpillars.

Karen goes into her garden one morning and finds the leaves covered in a sticky substance. What is this substance?

When the leaves sit in the sunshine they get hot and it makes them sweat.

What is a plasmid?

A high definition television

How is oxygen loaded, transported, and unloaded in the bloodstream?

Using a forklift

Explain the concept of homeostasis.

It is when you stay at home
all day and don't go out.

In the Hawaiian Islands there are around 500
different species of fruit fly. Give a reason for this.

There are approximately
500 varieties of fruit

Explain the word "genome."

It is an abbreviation of the two words: Gender and Gnome.

Draw a diagram to represent the human body and label the positions of all the major organs, including brain, heart, lungs, and kidneys.

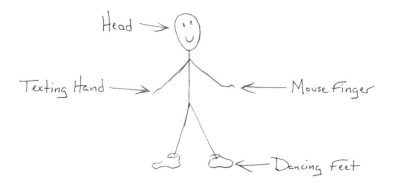

Draw a diagram indicating the location of the appendix.

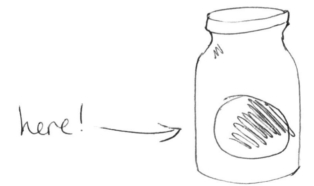

What is a cadaver?

It is a type of car.

What is a fossil?

A fossil is the remains of an extinct animal. The older the fossil, the more extinct the animal is.

What happens to your body when taking a breath?

Your chest gets bigger.

What is the world's largest living mammal?

The woolly mammoth

What happens when your body starts to age?

When you get old your organs work less effectively and you can become intercontinental.

State a type of fungus and explain one of its characteristic features.

The Bogey Man. He is green.

Below is a diagram of the heart. Please label the relevant sections.

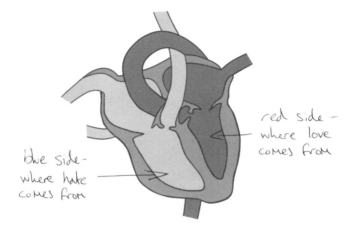

red side – where love comes from

blue side – where hate comes from

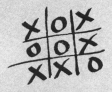

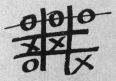

Subject: ....**Physics**........................

Steve is driving his car. He is traveling at 60 feet/second and the speed limit is 40 mph. Is Steve speeding?

He could find out by checking his speedometer.

Explain the word "momentum."

A brief moment

Explain the shape of the graph.

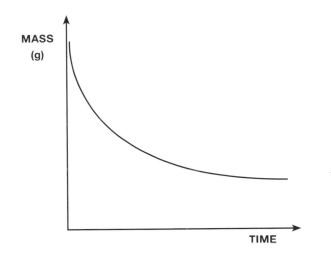

It curves, with a higher bit at the end and a rather aesthetically pleasing slope downwards towards a pretty flat straight bit. The actual graph itself consists of 2 straight lines meeting at the long left hard corner of the graph and moving away at a 90° angle. Each line has an arrow head on the end.

What was Sir Isaac Newton famous for?

He invented gravity.

Is the moon or the sun more important?

The Moon gives us light at night when we need it. The sun only provides light in the day when we don't. Therefore the moon is more important.

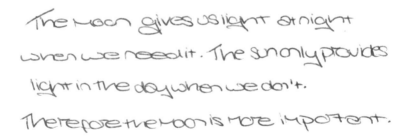

Write the first and second Laws of
Thermodynamics.

First rule of thermodynamics is you
do not talk about thermodynamics.

Second rule of thermodynamics is you
do not talk about thermodynamics.

Many people don't like eating radiation-treated food. How could a food scientist prove that radiation-treated food is safe?

By eating some!

Name an environmental side effect of burning fossil fuels.

Fire

Describe what happened during the "big bang."

A lot of noise.

Why do some researchers believe that living close to a cell phone tower might cause poor health?

You might walk into it.

Give the names of two gases that might contribute to global warming.

1. Bottom gas
2. Cow burps

Hannah sprays her new bike purple. The spraying of the bike gives it a negative charge and the paint a positive one. Why is this?

Positive – spraying is easier than using a paintbrush.

Negative – purple isn't a good colour for a bike.

Mobile phones are very popular. Give one advantage and one disadvantage of owning a mobile phone.

Advantage

You can order takeout for your school lunch.

Disadvantage

Your parents can get hold of you at any time.

What does a transformer do?

IT CAN GO FROM BEING A ROBOT TO A SPORTS CAR IN THREE SECONDS.

Give an example of a step-up transformer.

An exercise machine

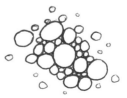

Give a reason why people would want to live near power lines.

You get your electricity faster.

Give three ways to reduce heat loss in your home.

1. Thermal underwear
2. Move to Hawaii
3. Close the door

When a star's life cycle is over there is a
possibility it will become a black hole.
Describe a "black hole."

Something very dark in the ground and
it looks like this

What instrument do you use to measure
temperature?

A trombone.

Describe the shape and structure of the Milky Way.

It's kind of like a long, bumpy rectangle.
It's completely covered in milk chocolate,
but inside there are two delicious layers:
chocolaty nougat and caramel.

2+2=5

Subject: Math

Change 7/8 to a decimal.

Name a regular triangle.

a three - sided triangle.

Find the angles marked with letters.

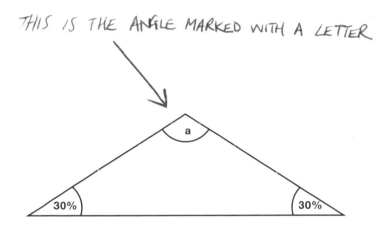

THIS IS THE ANGLE MARKED WITH A LETTER

a

30%

30%

To change centimeters to meters you _____.

take out centi.

Write two hundred thousand in figures.

two hundred thousand in figures.

What is a six-sided polygon known as?

a stop sign

There are 300 students in the 10th grade.
Mary and Mark want to find out the 10th grade's favorite color.
Mary asks 30 people.
Mark asks 150 people.
Mark says, "My conclusions are more likely to be reliable than Mary's."
Why does Mark think he is right?

Because Mark is a man

A car company is having a sale. A car that was $50,000 before the sale is now 30 percent off. What is the new price?

Still too expensive.

Name an angle complementary to BDC

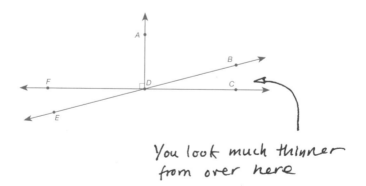

You look much thinner from over here

BANANA CAR

Construct a ~~rectangle with sides Y and ends Z.~~

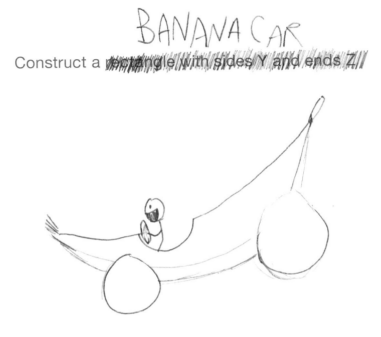

I want to retake this test.

Expand $2(x + y)$

$$2(x+y)$$

$$2(x + y)$$

$$2(x + y)$$

$$2(x + y)$$

Simplify the following equation.

$$\sqrt{\frac{5}{5}} \qquad \frac{\sqrt{5}}{5} = \sqrt{}$$

x is inversely proportional to the square of y.
x=3 and y=4
Express x in terms of y.

$$:-x + :-y = :-)$$

What is conditional probability?

Maybe, maybe not

What is the splitting formula?

boy meets girl → boy meets another girl
→ girl finds out about other girl
= the splitting formula.
This is not to be confused with the spitting
formula, that's just antisocial.

What is a random variable?

Someone with multiple personalities

What is a discrete random variable?
Give an example with your answer.

It is a person that hides in the corner at parties, similar to the wall flower but a bit more unpredictable after a few drinks.

You are at a friend's party. Six cupcakes are distributed among nine plates, and there is no more than one cake per plate. What is the probability of receiving a plate with a cake on it?

None, if my sister is invited too.

What is the symbol for pi?

← pi!

John and Julie are both good badminton players.
Is it more probable that Julie will beat John in four
games out of seven or five games out of nine?

She will win every game.
She is a girl - girls are
better at these things.

How should Julie play to minimize any loss?

Dirty!

Carl Gossell is a machinist. He bought some new machinery for about $125,000. He wants to calculate the value of the machinery over the next 10 years for tax purposes. If the machinery depreciates at the rate of 15% per year, what is the value of the machinery (to the nearest $100) at the end of the 10 years?

$0. It will be stolen by rats by then.

A new car costs $32,000. It is expected to depreciate 12% each year for 4 years and then depreciate 8% each year thereafter. Find the value of the car in 6 years.

No one will drive cars in 6 years with fuel going up like it is.

The population of Bulgaria has been decreasing at an annual rate of 1.3%. If the population of Bulgaria was about 7,797,000 in the year 2000, predict its population in the year 2010.

0. There will be a cheesecake shortage.

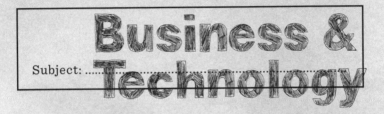

Subject: Business & Technology

Explain the phrase "free press."

When your mom irons
pants for you.

Explain the word "wholesaler."

Someone who sells you whole
items, e.g. a whole cake.

What is a desktop?

Where you do your work

What do you use to navigate a desktop?

A map and a compass

Paul frequently uses the Internet to research information. Suggest two items of information Paul could locate on the Internet that might help him in running his business.

Item 1: www. how-to-run-a-business. com

Item 2: www. how-not-to-run-a-business. com

Suggest three steps Paul is likely to take when selecting the best candidate for a job.

Step one: You're hired

Step two: You're fired

Step three: You're hired

Describe the term "stakeholder."

A vampire hunter.
Buffy being the most famous

Hugo King is an engineer. He is a sole trader.
Explain the business term "sole trader."

It means he has sold his sole
to the devil!

John's net pay is $150. His deductions are $38.

a) Work out John's gross pay.

The money he spends on porn magazines every week.

b) State one mandatory deduction from John's pay.

Beer

c) State one voluntary deduction John may or may not pay.

Tax

Claire used good body language at a job interview. Can you think of three examples of good body language that Claire may have used?

1. *pole dancing*

2. *The moonwalk*

3. *The Bolero*

Claire was well prepared for her interview. Explain how Claire may have prepared herself for the interview.

Had a bath and put on her lucky pants.

Jeff has been asked to collect data about the amount of television his friends watch. Think of an appropriate question he could ask them.

How much TV do you watch?

What guarantees might a mortgage company insist on when buying a house?

They may check to see whether you are well endowed before allowing the purchase.

What is a "partnership'?

A Ship that takes two people to drive

What happens during a census?

During the census a man goes from door to door and increases the population.

What is a computer virus?

An S.T.D.
A systematically Transmitted Disease.

Joanna works in an office. Her computer is
a stand-alone system. What is a stand-alone
computer system?

It doesn't come with
a chair

What is hacking?

A really bad cough

What is malware?

It is badly made clothing

What is a CD-ROM?

An album of romantic music.

What is a hard disk?

It doesn't break when you put it in the dishwasher.

What is a floppy disk?

It is a disk that has been left at in the rain

What is a network?

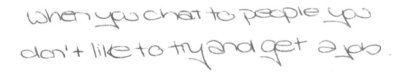

When you chat to people you don't like to try and get a job.

I think, therefore...

Subject: ......................

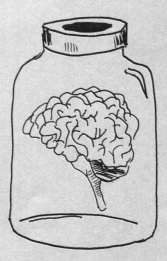

Describe what is meant by "forgetting."

I can't remember

Freud stated that the superego contains the moral aspect of one's personality. Define the term "superego."

A toaster waffle that wears a cape and fights crime!

Explain the "psychodynamic approach."

Using your Mind to Move things
like a jedi

Suggest a way to abate aggression.

If your hands are tied behind
your back you can't punch people

Explain the process of "learning."

A process by which information goes into one ear and out of the other.

Express the term "stereotype."

It is the kind of CD player you own.

What does the phrase "case study' mean?

It is a process whereby you sit and stare at your suitcase before you go on a trip but not knowing what to pack.

Who said, "I think, therefore I am"?

I did.

Using your knowledge of Freud, provide an example of when a dream represents Freud's theory.

If you dream about cookies it means you are subconciously thinking about sex, but If you are dreaming about sex, it means you are thinking about cookies.

Please fill in the sections of Maslow's Hierarchy of Needs below.

Subject: ....

UH
OH

Explain the dispersal of various farming types in the Midwest.

The cows + pigs are distributed in different fields so they don't eat each other

Explain what is meant by the term "pastoral farming."

It's a farm run by reverends.

Define the phrase "commercial farming."

It is when a farmer advertises his farm on T.V to get more customers.

Define the phrase "subsistence farming."

It's when a farmer doesn't get any assistance

Define the term "intensive farming."

It is when a farmer never has a day off.

Explain the meaning of the word "magma."

Japanese cartoons.

What scale do seismologists use to measure the force of earthquakes?

A very strong one
(not glass).

Volcanoes occur on what kind of plate margins?

Hot plates.

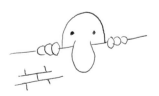

What happens at the edge of a destructive plate margin?

It breaks!

"Powerful aftershocks rocked the city, fires burned out of control, streets were full of debris and ruined buildings. At least 30 people were injured." Which type of natural disaster is being described in the report?

The end of American Idol

Name the area of calm at the center of a storm.

The pie in the sky.

What does the word "lava" mean?

A pre-pubescent caterpillar

THIS WAY

What do we call a person forced to leave their home, perhaps by a natural disaster or war, without having another home to go to?

Homeless 😐

Explain the word "migration."

A migration is a bad headache.

Define the phrase "heavy industry."

An industry that sells tons.

Which artificial waterway runs between the Mediterranean and Red Seas?

The Sewage Canal.

What was the main industry in Persia?

Cats

The race of people known as Malays come from which country?

Malaria

Name the smaller rivers that run into the Nile.

The Juveniles.

Name six animals that live specifically in the Arctic.

Two polar bears
~~Three~~ Four seals

Inhabitants of Moscow are called . . .

Mosquitoes

Name one of the primary products of the Hawaiian Islands.

Grass skirts and flower necklaces

What is the collective name given to the
inhabitants of the Philippine Islands?

The Philistines

Name one famous Greek landmark.

The most famous Greek
landmark is the Apocalypse

Name two animals native to Siberia.

The lynx and the larynx

Where was the Declaration of Independence signed?

At the bottom.

How high is Mount Everest?

Depends how much snowfall it has had since it was last measured.

The Narmada and the Tapi river valleys are said to be old rift valleys. What is a rift valley?

Valleys that have fallen out after an argument.

Why was the Berlin Wall built?

Germany was competing with China.

Summarize the major events of the Cold War.

It started off by someone throwing an ice cream + then someone threw a popsicle back.

What were the consequences of the Cold War?

Everyone got really hot what with all that running, fighting in the snow with snowballs and riding horses pulling sleds. No wonder Santa Claus has rosy red cheeks.

Who were the Bolsheviks?

People led by linen

Explain the word "autocracy."

A country that has lots of cars.

Explain what is meant by the word "dictator."

Someone who reads
out loud

Upon ascending the throne the first thing Queen
Elizabeth II did was to . . .

sit down

What was the largest threat to world peace in the 1980s?

Heavy metal, because it was very loud.

Summarize the key developments of the Industrial Revolution.

Industry revolved

What does the Statue of Liberty represent?

A green lady holding up a large glass of wine. She is wearing a crown. She is the Queen of America.

Name two of the classes that existed in medieval England.

History class &
Geography class

Who was Socrates?

Socrates was a famous old greek teacher who went around giving people advice. They Killed him. He later died from an overdose of wedlock which is apparently poisonous. After his death, his career suffered a dramatic decline.

Who wrote *The Republic* and *The Apology*?

Playdoh.

Describe the differences between the February
Revolution and the October Revolution.

One occurred in February
and one occurred in October.

What is the significance of an altar?

God knows!

What is having only one spouse called?

Monotony

What do Christians celebrate at Christmas?

When Joseph and Mary had a baby called
Jesus. They travelled to Bethlehem
by plane and Pontius was their pilot.

What were Jesus' closest group of followers
known as?

The 12 decibels

What miracle do Christians celebrate at Easter time?

Chocolate!

State two major world religions.

1. The Force in Star Wars

2. Football

What is the difference between the New Testament and the Old Testament?

The New Testament was a better version.

What is a pilgrimage?

It's when lots of people wander off in the same direction for no apparent reason

Name one of the early Romans' greatest achievements.

Learning to speak Latin.

Name the successor of the first Roman emperor.

The Second Roman Emperor

Who was Solomon?

He was a very popular man
who had Too wives and
300 porcupines

What were the circumstances of Julius Caesar's death?

Suspicious ones

Where was Hadrian's Wall built?

Around Hadrians garden

What is Sir Francis Drake known for?

Sir Francis Drake circumsized the world with a 100 foot clipper.

Name the wife of Orpheus, whom he attempted to save from the underworld.

Mrs Orpheus

Who was it that helped Theseus escape from the Labyrinth?

David Bowie

Name one of Abraham Lincoln's greatest achievements.

Having his pace carved in rock

What did Mahatma Gandhi and Genghis Khan have in common?

Unusual names

What is Karl Marx known for?

karl marx was one of the marx Brothers.

Discuss the style of *Romeo and Juliet.*

It is written entirely in Islamic pentameter. The play is full of heroic couplets, one example being Romeo + Juliet themselves

How does Romeo's character develop throughout the play?

It doesn't, it's just self, self, self, all the way through.

How much is Romeo to blame for what happens at the end of *Romeo and Juliet*?

He is completely to blame.
He's an alpha male and
he's named after a car.

Use the word "judicious" in a sentence to illustrate its meaning.

I am using "judicious" in this sentence to illustrate it's meaning

Writing Prompt: Imagine you work for a travel agent. Describe a place you have been to and explain why it would interest someone of a similar age.

My mom and dad drag me to my grandparents place in New Jersey every year. I wouldn't recommend it to anyone my age.

Why should we be optimistic about the future? Use either a discursive or an argumentative style in composing your answer.

Because if you're not positive about the future then you ain't got much hope have you.

In *Pride and Prejudice*, at what moment does Elizabeth Bennet realize her true feelings for Mr. Darcy?

When she sees him coming out of the lake.

Explain the saying: Some people don't look up until they are flat on their backs.

Some people can't look up because something has happened to their necks. For example, if a person gets kicked in the neck by a kung-fu midget, they will not be able to look up.

Use the word "doldrums" in a sentence.

I can not play the doldrums.

Use the word "congenial" in a sentence.

When you leave the gravy out too long, it congenials.

Suggest an appropriate word for each of these meanings:

a.) An appliance or implement designed to help one do work.

My parents and the Internet

b.) To be on water without sinking

Jesus

c.) Aggressive; harsh

My brother and my teacher Mrs Topley

d.) Faultless or highly skilled

My answers!

F

Try
Harder